Piano • Vocal • Guitar

LOVE BALLADS

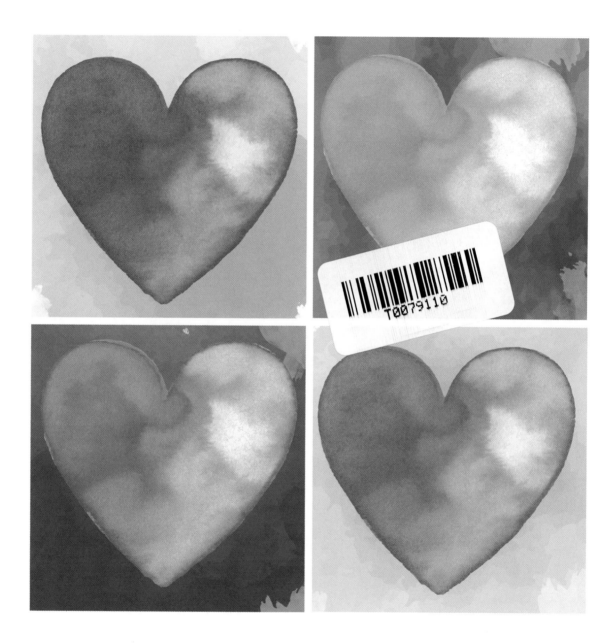

ISBN 978-1-5400-7034-0

HAL•LEONARD®

For all works contained herein:
Unauthorized copying, arranging, adapting, recording, Internet posting, public performance,
or other distribution of the music in this publication is an infringement of copyright.
Infringers are liable under the law.

Visit Hal Leonard Online at
www.halleonard.com

Contact us:
Hal Leonard
7777 West Bluemound Road
Milwaukee, WI 53213
Email: info@halleonard.com

In Europe, contact:
Hal Leonard Europe Limited
42 Wigmore Street
Marylebone, London, W1U 2RN
Email: info@halleonardeurope.com

In Australia, contact:
Hal Leonard Australia Pty. Ltd.
4 Lentara Court
Cheltenham, Victoria, 3192 Australia
Email: info@halleonard.com.au

CONTENTS

AGAINST ALL ODDS
(Take a Look at Me Now)
from AGAINST ALL ODDS

Words and Music by
PHIL COLLINS

Moderately slow

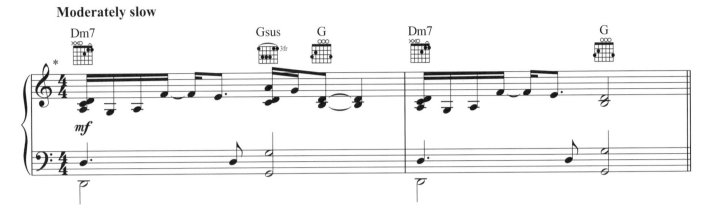

How can I just let you walk a-way, just let you leave with-out ___ a trace, when I

stand here tak-ing ev-'ry breath ___ with you? ___ Ooh. ___ You're the

* *Recorded a half step lower.*

on - ly one who real - ly knew me ___ at all. ___

How can you just walk a - way from me, when all I can do is watch you leave? _ 'Cause we've
wish I could just make you turn a - round, turn a - round and see me cry. ___ There's so

shared the laugh - ter and ___ the pain, ___ and e - ven shared ___ the tears. ___ You're the
much I need ___ to say ___ to you, _ so man - y rea - sons why. ___

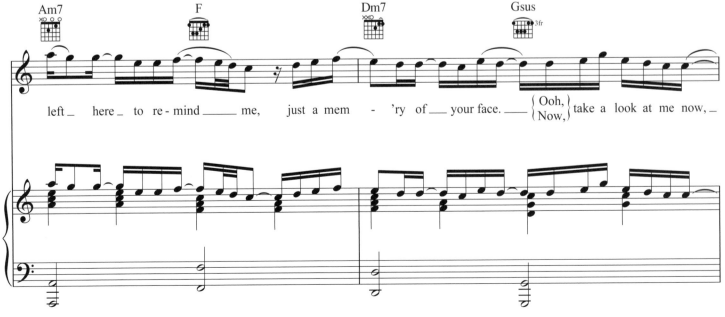

ALL OUT OF LOVE

Words and Music by GRAHAM RUSSELL
and CLIVE DAVIS

Moderately

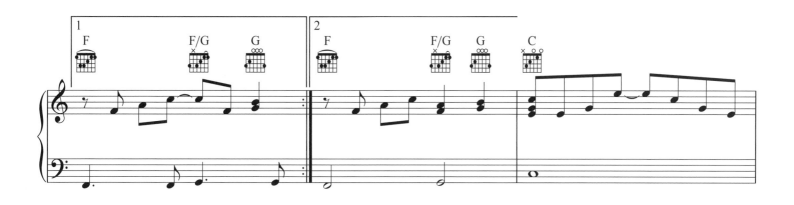

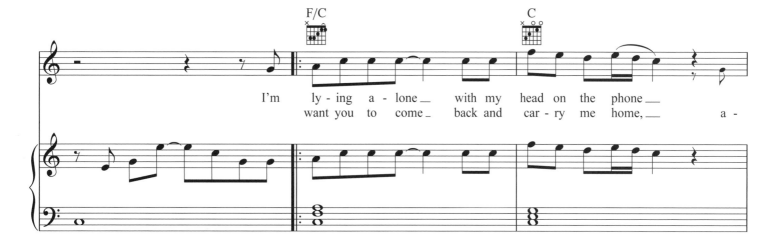

I'm ly-ing a-lone _ with my head on the phone _
want you to come _ back and car-ry me home, _ a-

think-ing of you _ 'til it hurts. _
way from these long, _ lone-ly nights. _

I know you hurt, too, _ but what
I'm reach-ing for you. _ Are you

ALL OF ME

Words and Music by JOHN STEPHENS
and TOBY GAD

BEST PART OF ME

Words and Music by ED SHEERAN,
BENJAMIN LEVIN and ABBEY SMITH

Male: My lungs are black, _ my heart is pure. _

My hands _ are scarred _ from nights _ be-fore.

BEAUTIFUL CRAZY

Words and Music by ROBERT WILLIFORD,
LUKE COMBS and WYATT DURRETTE

Slow Country Ballad, in 2

starts with a cof - fee and ends with a wine. Takes for - ev - er get - ting read - y, so she's

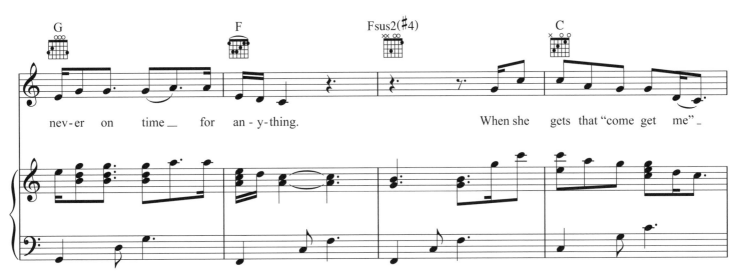

nev - er on time _ for an - y - thing. When she gets that "come get me" _

* Recorded a half step lower.

EVERMORE
from BEAUTY AND THE BEAST

Music by ALAN MENKEN
Lyrics by TIM RICE

GROW AS WE GO

Words and Music by BEN ABRAHAM,
ALEX HOPE and BEN PLATT

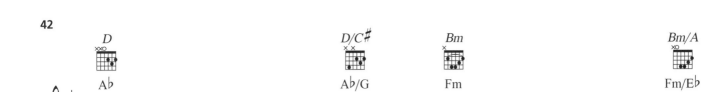

You say you'd rath-er be ___ a - lone, ___

'cause you think you won't find __ it tied to some-one else. ___

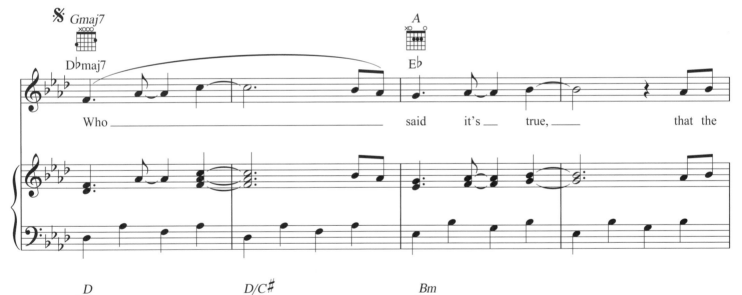

Who _____ said it's __ true, _____ that the

grow - ing on - ly hap - pens on your own? They

HAVE I TOLD YOU LATELY

Words and Music by
VAN MORRISON

Slowly, with expression

Have I told____ you late-ly that I love you? Have I told you there's no one else____ a-bove____ you?

Fill my heart____ with glad-ness, take a-way all____ my sad-ness,

JUST THE WAY YOU ARE

Words and Music by
BILLY JOEL

HEAVEN

Words and Music by BRYAN ADAMS
and JIM VALLANCE

I CAN'T MAKE YOU LOVE ME

Words and Music by MIKE REID
and ALLEN SHAMBLIN

Turn down the lights, turn down the bed,

turn down these voic - es in - side my head. Lay down with me,

72

I GET TO LOVE YOU

Words and Music by MAGGIE ECKFORD
and MATT BRONLEEWE

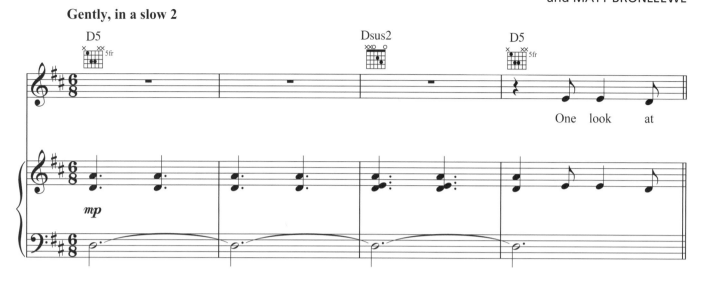

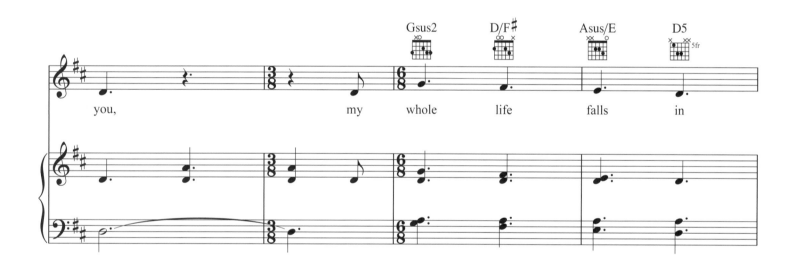

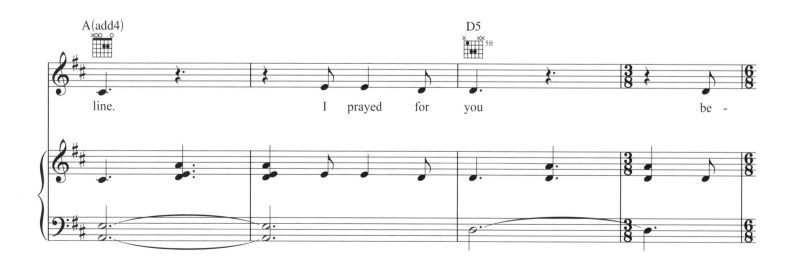

I WANT TO KNOW WHAT LOVE IS

Words and Music by
MICK JONES

I'LL NEVER LOVE AGAIN

from A STAR IS BORN

Words and Music by STEFANI GERMANOTTA,
AARON RAITIERE, HILLARY LINDSEY
and NATALIE HEMBY

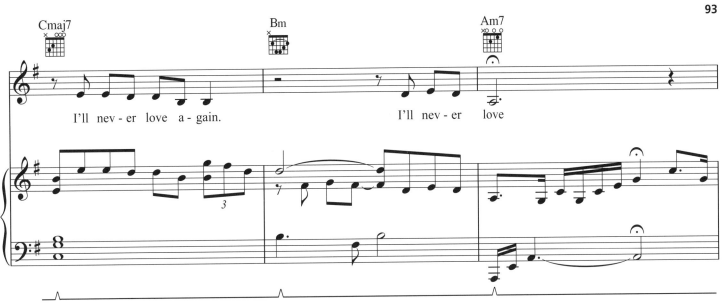

I'll nev-er love a-gain. I'll nev-er love

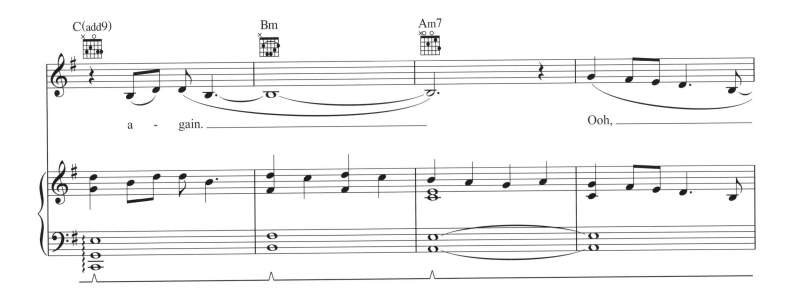

a - gain. _____ Ooh, _____

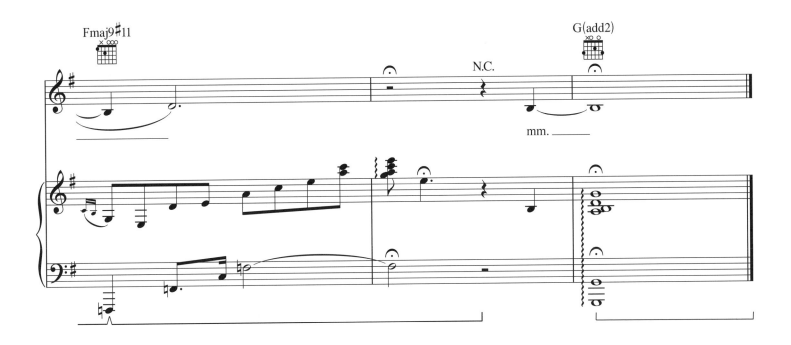

mm. _____

LOVE OF MY LIFE

Words and Music by
FREDDIE MERCURY

Love of my life, ___ you've hurt ___ me.
Love of my life, ___ don't leave ___ me.

You've bro-ken my heart ___ and
You've tak-en my love; ___ and you

now you leave me.
now de-sert me.

Love of my life, ___ can't you see?

Bring it

LOVE SOMEONE

Words and Music by LUKAS FORCHHAMMER,
MORTEN RISTORP, MORTEN PILEGAARD,
JARAMYE DANIELS, DON STEFANO,
DAVID LaBREL and JAMES GHALEB

There are days _____   I wake up and I
When you say _____   you love the way I

pinch my-self.   You're with me, not some-one else.
make you feel,   ev-'ry-thing be-comes so real.

And I'm scared, _ yeah, I'm _ still scared _   that it's
Don't be scared, _ no, don't _ be scared, _   'cause you're

LOVER

Words and Music by
TAYLOR SWIFT

lov- er.

We could let our friends crash in the liv - ing room. _

This is our place; we make the call. _ I'm

high - ly sus - pi - cious that ev - 'ry-one who sees you wants _ you. _ I've

NEVER ENOUGH

from THE GREATEST SHOWMAN

Words and Music by BENJ PASEK
and JUSTIN PAUL

PERFECT

Words and Music by
ED SHEERAN

Classic Ballad

I found a love ___ for ___ me. ___

Dar-ling, just dive ___ right in, fol-low my

lead. Well, I found a girl, ___ beau-ti-

118

you look per-fect to-night."

Ba - by, _____ I'm _____ danc-ing in the

dark with you be-tween my arms. Bare-foot on the

REMEDY

Words and Music by ADELE ADKINS
and RYAN TEDDER

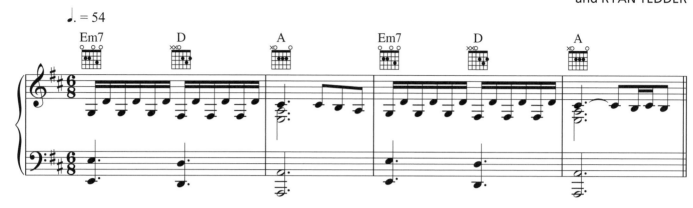

1. I re-mem-ber all of the things that I thought I want-ed to be.
2. No riv-er is too wide or too deep for me to swim to

you. So des-p'rate to find a way out of my
Come what-ev - er, I'll be the shel-ter that

Em7 D A Em7 D
world and fi - nal - ly breathe. Right be - fore my eyes I
won't let the rain come through. Your love, it is my
A Em7 D A G
saw, my heart it came to life. This ain't eas - y, it's not meant
truth and I will al - ways love you, love you.
1° only
A/G Em/G
to be. Ev - 'ry sto - ry has it's scars but when the
When the
D A Em Bm
pain cuts you deep, and when the night keeps you from sleep - ing, just

RIGHT HERE WAITING

Words and Music by
RICHARD MARX

O- ceans a- part, _____ day af- ter day, _____ and I
I took for grant - ed all the times _____ that I

F G C G
here wait - ing for you.
What-ev - er it takes,
or how my heart breaks,
Am F G
To Coda
1
Am
I will be right here wait - ing for you.
2
Fsus2/D C/E F(add2)
3fr
I won-der how we can sur - vive
this ro - mance.
Fsus2/D C/E F(add2) Gsus G/B
3fr
But in the end, if I'm with you,
I'll take the chance.

SAY YOU WON'T LET GO

Words and Music by STEVEN SOLOMON,
JAMES ARTHUR and NEIL ORMANDY

Moderate Ballad

I met you in the dark, you lit me up,
I wake you up with some break-fast in bed,

you made me feel as though I was e-nough. __
I'll bring you cof-fee with a kiss on your head. __
We danced the night a-way,
And I'll take the kids to school,

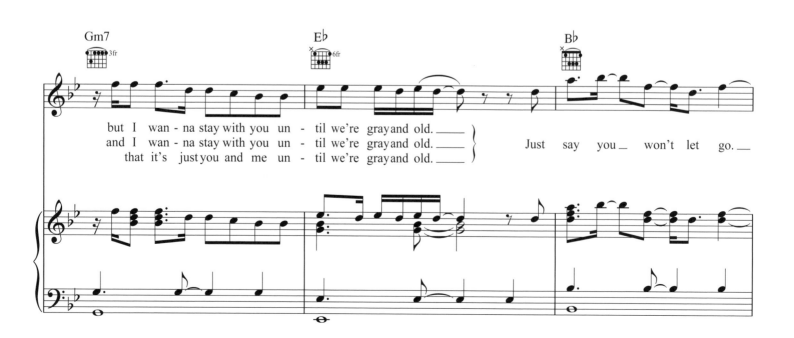

Just say you __ won't __ let go. _____

I wan - na live with you   e - ven when we're ghosts, __

'cause you were al - ways there   for me when   I   need - ed you most. _____

say you __ won't __ let go. _____ Just

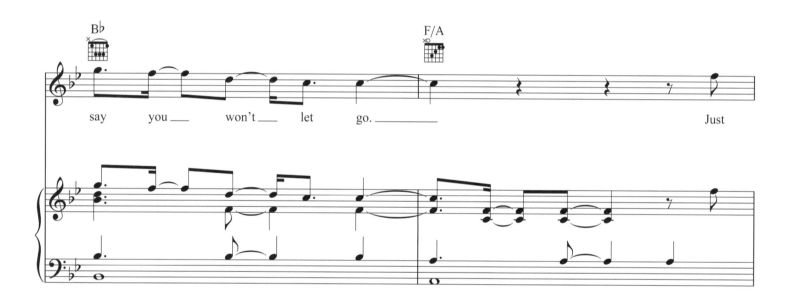

say you __ won't __ let go. _____ Just

say you __ won't __ let go. _____

LOVE IS ALIVE

Words and Music by NATHAN CHAPMAN
and CHANTAL KREVIAZUK

SOMEONE YOU LOVED

Words and Music by LEWIS CAPALDI,
BENJAMIN KOHN, PETER KELLEHER,
THOMAS BARNES and SAMUEL ROMAN

Moderate Ballad

With pedal

I'm go-ing un-der, and this time I fear there's no one to save __
I'm go-ing un-der, and this time I fear there's no one to turn __

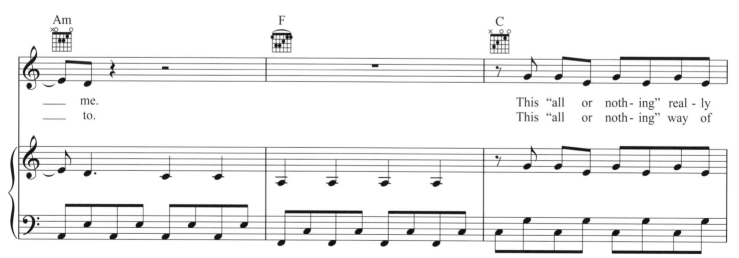

__ me.   This "all or noth-ing" real-ly
__ to.   This "all or noth-ing" way of

* *Recorded a half step higher.*

WHERE DO BROKEN HEARTS GO

Words and Music by CHUCK JACKSON
and FRANK WILDHORN

SPEECHLESS

Words and Music by DAN SMYERS,
SHAY MOONEY, JORDAN REYNOLDS
and LAURA VELTZ

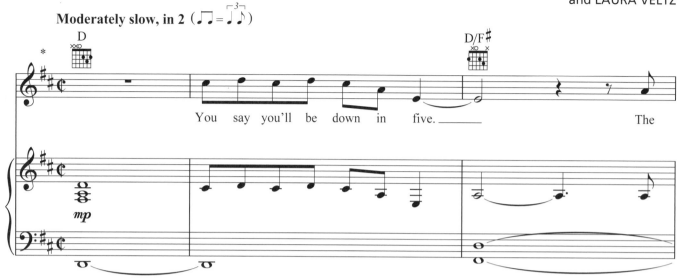

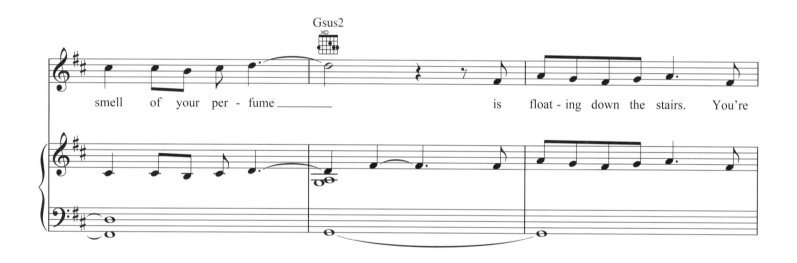

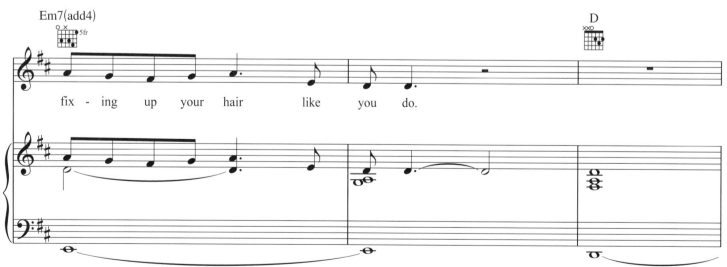

* Recorded a half step lower.

A THOUSAND YEARS

from the Summit Entertainment film THE TWILIGHT SAGA: BREAKING DAWN – PART 1

Words and Music by DAVID HODGES
and CHRISTINA PERRI

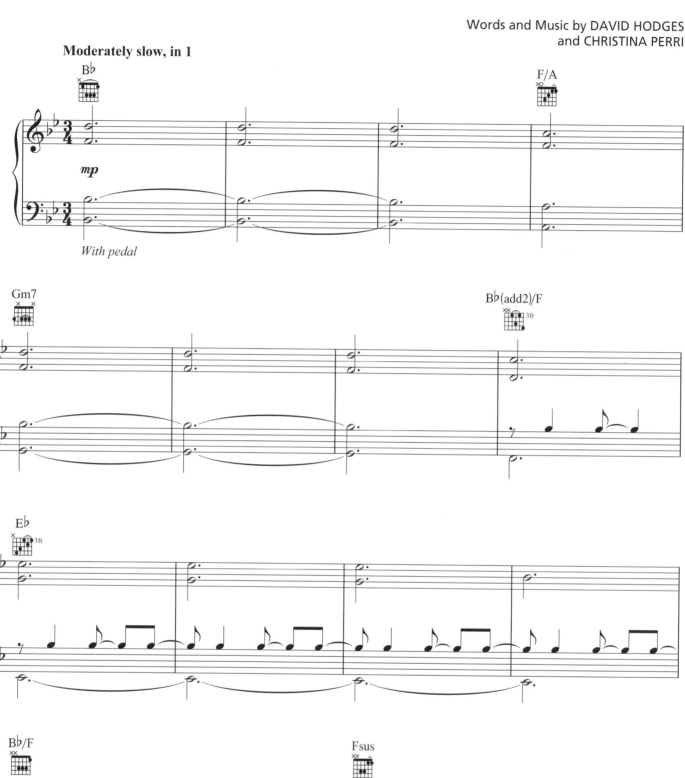

B♭maj7/F
F7sus
F(add4)
Cm11
Gm7
One
step
clos
-
F(add4)
Cm11
er.
One
F
Gm7
F(add4)/A
F(add4)
D.S. al Coda
(take 2nd ending)
step
clos
-
er.

YOU'RE THE INSPIRATION

Words and Music by PETER CETERA
and DAVID FOSTER

1. You know our love was meant to be ___
2. *(See additional lyrics)*

the kind of love ___ that lasts ___ for-

ev - er. ___ And I want you here with

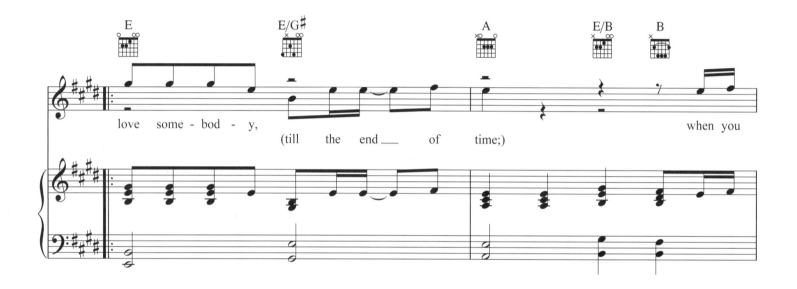

Additional Lyrics

2. And I know (yes, I know)
That it's plain to see
We're so in love when we're together.
Now I know (now I know)
That I need you here with me
From tonight until the end of time.
You should know everywhere I go;
Always on my mind, you're in my heart, in my soul.
Chorus

YOU ARE THE REASON

Words and Music by CALUM SCOTT,
COREY SANDERS and JONATHAN MAGUIRE

YOUR SONG

Words and Music by ELTON JOHN
and BERNIE TAUPIN

THE MOST ROMANTIC MUSIC IN THE WORLD
ARRANGED FOR PIANO, VOICE, AND GUITAR

The Best Love Songs Ever – 2nd Edition

This revised edition includes 65 romantic favorites: Always • Beautiful in My Eyes • Can You Feel the Love Tonight • Endless Love • Have I Told You Lately • Misty • Something • Through the Years • Truly • When I Fall in Love • and more.

00359198 .... $19.99

The Best Wedding Songs Ever – 2nd Edition

70 favorite songs of love and commitment are featured in this updated second edition of this popular wedding songbook. Songs include: All I Ask of You • Bridal Chorus • Can't Help Falling in Love • Canon in D • Endless Love • (Everything I Do) I Do It for You • From This Moment On • Here and Now • I Will Always Love You • Jesu, Joy of Man's Desiring • Just the Way You Are • The Lord's Prayer • Marry You • Open Arms • Perfect • Trumpet Voluntary • Wedding March • Wonderful Tonight • You Raise Me Up • and more.

Listen to a Spotify playlist of all the songs featured in this book!

00290985 .... $24.99

The Big Book of Love Songs – 3nd Edition

82 romantic favorites in many musical styles: Bless the Broken Road • Endless Love • Fields of Gold • How Deep Is Your Love • Just the Way You Are • Lady in Red • The Nearness of You • Only You • The Power of Love • Thinking Out Loud • Unchained Melody • and more.

00257807 .... $22.99

The Bride's Wedding Music Collection

A great collection of popular, classical and sacred songs for wedding musicians or engaged couples who are planning their service. Over 40 categorized songs, plus a website to hear audio clips! Songs include: Bless the Broken Road • Canon in D • Everything • Grow Old with Me • In My Life • Jesu, Joy of Man's Desiring • The Lord's Prayer • Marry Me • Ode to Joy • When You Say Nothing at All • and more.

00312298 .... $19.99

HAL•LEONARD®
www.halleonard.com

The Bride's Guide to Wedding Music – 2nd Edition

This great guide is a complete resource for planning wedding music. It includes a thorough article on choosing music for a wedding ceremony, and 65 songs in many different styles to satisfy lots of different tastes. The songs are grouped by categories, including preludes, processionals, recessionals, traditional sacred songs, popular songs, country songs, contemporary Christian songs, Broadway numbers and new age piano music.

00310615 .... $19.95

Disney Love Songs – 3rd Edition

20 heartfelt Disney classic songs are featured in the third edition of this collection. Includes arrangements for piano, voice and guitar of: Beauty and the Beast • Candle on the Water • A Dream Is a Wish Your Heart Makes • Evermore • I See the Light • Kiss the Girl • Love Is an Open Door • True Love's Kiss • When She Loved Me • and more.

00283395 .... $16.99

Love Songs
Budget Books Series

74 favorite love songs, including: And I Love Her • Cherish • Crazy • Endless Love • Fields of Gold • I Just Called to Say I Love You • I'll Be There • (You Make Me Feel Like) A Natural Woman • Wonderful Tonight • You Are So Beautiful • and more.

00310834 .... $12.99

Modern Love Songs

27 recent hits, including: Just a Kiss (Lady Antebellum) • Just the Way You Are (Bruno Mars) • Love Somebody (Maroon 5) • Marry Me (Train) • No One (Alicia Keys) • Ours (Taylor Swift) • Stay (Rihanna) • A Thousand Years (Christina Perri) • Unconditionally (Katy Perry) • Wanted (Hunter Hayes) • and more.

00127068 .... $17.99

The Modern Wedding Collection

Piano solo arrangements of 21 beautiful current hits, including: All of Me • Everything • God Gave Me You • I Won't Give Up • Just the Way You Are • Love Me Like You Do • Love Story • The Luckiest • No One • One and Only • Thinking Out Loud • A Thousand Years • The Way I Am • We Found Love • You're Beautiful • and more.

00151783 .... $14.99

Modern Wedding Songs – 2nd Edition

27 contemporary favorites for today's couples: All of Me • Can't Stop the Feeling • I Choose You • Love Someone • Marry You • Perfect • Say You Won't Let Go • Thinking Out Loud • A Thousand Years • Yours • and more.

00254368 .... $17.99

Romance – Boleros Favoritos

Features 48 Spanish and Latin American favorites: Aquellos Ojos Verdes • Bésame Mucho • El Reloj • Frenes • Inolvidable • La Vida Es Un Sueño • Perfidia • Siempre En Mi Corazón • Solamente Una Vez • and more.

00310383 .... $17.99

Romantic Sheet Music Collection

Over 30 songs perfect for expressing that loving feeling, including: At Last • Can't Help Falling in Love • Crazy Love • First Day of My Life • I Just Called to Say I Love You • In Your Eyes • Let's Stay Together • Maybe I'm Amazed • Sea of Love • Thinking Out Loud • Unchained Melody • Your Song • and more.

00148757 .... $17.99

Songs from the Heart

40 songs about love and friendship, including: Annie's Song • Don't Know Much • Endless Love • Faithfully • Hello • I Will Always Love You • I'll Have to Say I Love You in a Song • Just the Way You Are • Longer • More Than Words • Right Here Waiting • That's What Friends Are For • The Wind Beneath My Wings • and more.

00121512 .... $17.99

Today's Hits for Weddings

Contains 25 of today's best pop and country hits that are perfect for weddings! Includes: Bless the Broken Road • Everything • Halo • I Do • Just the Way You Are • Love Story • Lucky • Marry Me • Mine • River of Love • Today Was a Fairytale • You Raise Me Up • and more.

00312316 .... $16.99

Valentine

Let your love light shine with this collection of 50 romantic favorites! Includes: Can't Help Falling and Love • Endless Love • If • Just the Way You Are • L-O-V-E • Mona Lisa • My Funny Valentine • Something • Three Coins in the Fountain • We've Only Just Begun • You Are So Beautiful • You'll Accomp'ny Me • and more.

00310977 .... $16.95